Hitch your wagon to a star.

Ralph Waldo Emerson

Presented to:

_____

Presented by:

_____

One on One with Graduates . . . A Prayer Book for Graduates
©2006 Elm Hill Books
ISBN: 1404186522

This manuscript written and compiled by Christy Phillippe, Barbara Scott, and Rebecca Currington in association with Snapdragon Editorial Group, Inc.

Cover and interior pages designed by D/SR Design, LLC.

One on One with God . . .

A Prayer Book for Graduates

Elm Hill Books
An Imprint of J. Countryman®

An old hymn goes: "What a friend we have in Jesus, all our sins and griefs to bear. What a privilege to carry everything to God in prayer." They're wonderful words, aren't they—comforting, strengthening, liberating. And they are words of truth! In the Bible, God invites us into friendship with Him, urging us to cast all our cares on Him. Have you ever thought about talking to God as you would to a friend?

One on One with God . . . A Prayer Book for Graduates was designed to guide and inspire you as you reach out to God in friendship and converse with Him concerning the issues, activities, and relationships that will impact you as you take your first steps into a new phase of your life. Think of these written prayers as letters to your best friend—God. Make them your own by adding the names of family and friends and specific needs. And don't forget to record and date your answers. God bless you as you embark on this exciting spiritual adventure.

One on One with God . . .

A Prayer Book for Graduates

Table of Contents

Daily Prayers for . . .

Daily Prayers for Help . . .

Daily Prayers for Guidance . . .

Daily Prayers of Praise for . . .

God of all goodness, grant us to desire ardently, to seek wisely, to know surely, and to accomplish perfectly Thy holy will, for the glory of Thy name.

SAINT THOMAS AQUINAS

Daily Prayers . . .

Daily Prayer . . . for salvation

*God our Savior saved us—not because we were good
enough to be saved but because of his kindness and pity—
by washing away our sins and giving us the new
joy of the indwelling Holy Spirit.*
TITUS 3:4–5 TLB

Dear Heavenly Father,

I've been working so hard at school, ignoring You and all the wonderful things You have done for me. I'm so sorry for all the ways I have offended You. Please forgive me of my sins and accept me as Your child, a member of Your family.

I believe that Jesus died for me—that even if I were the only person on earth, He still would have gone to the cross to save me. Thank You for this amazing gift of salvation. I want to follow You for the rest of my life. I want You to be part of everything I do from this day forward. Help me to live a life that is pleasing to You—in every way.

Amen.

*Salvation that comes from trusting Christ—
which is the message we preach—is within easy reach.*
ROMANS 10:8 NLT

A man may go to heaven without health, without riches, without honors, without learning, without friends, but he can never go there without Christ.

John Dyer

MY PERSONAL PRAYER

Dear Father:

_____

_____

_____

_____

_____

_____

_____

_____

Amen

God is ready to help you right now.
Today is the day of salvation.
2 CORINTHIANS 6:2 NLT

Salvation is found in no one else, for there is
no other name under heaven given to men
by which we must be saved.
ACTS 4:12 NIV

Daily Prayer . . . for peace

God's peace is far more wonderful than the human mind can understand. His peace will guard your hearts and minds as you live in Christ Jesus.
PHILIPPIANS 4:7 NLT

Dear Heavenly Father,

So much stuff is happening in my life right now—so many changes taking place—and I often worry about the outcome. My mind whirls with the opportunities I see after graduation and the choices I need to make.

I need Your peace, Lord. Please help me to rest in You and know deep within my heart that You are in complete control of everything that happens to me. Teach me to trust that You know what's best for me and that You are holding me in the palm of Your hand.

Thank You for the *peace that passes all understanding*—the peace that knows my future is safe with You.

Amen.

Jesus said, "Peace I leave with you; my peace I give you. I do not give to you as the world gives. Do not let your hearts be troubled and do not be afraid."
JOHN 14:27 NIV

Where there is peace, God is.

George Herbert

MY PERSONAL PRAYER

Dear Father:

_____

_____

_____

_____

_____

_____

_____

Amen

The LORD blesses his people with peace.
PSALM 29:11 NIV

*May the Lord himself, who is our source of peace,
give you peace at all times and in every way.*
2 THESSALONIANS 3:16 GNT

Daily Prayer . . . for joy

Weeping may endure for a night,
but joy comes in the morning.
PSALM 30:5

Dear Heavenly Father,

Please fill me with Your divine joy. I want to experience more than just temporary happiness— happiness that always depends on whether life is on an upswing. Even the pleasure of graduating will fade with time. I want to know the deeper joy that comes from a close, long-lasting relationship with You.

Only when my life is anchored in Your love will my joy endure regardless of the circumstances. And that's the kind of joy I want—steady and enduring. When Your joy is reflected in my life, I'll have something to offer others. A smile on a dreary day. A word of encouragement. A song when the storm is raging. Thank You, Lord, for a heart full of divine joy.

Amen.

God will give beauty for ashes, joy instead
of mourning, praise instead of despair.
ISAIAH 61:3 NLT

Joy is the echo of God's life in us.

Joseph Marmion

MY PERSONAL PRAYER

Dear Father:

_____

_____

_____

_____

_____

_____

_____

Amen

I'm whistling, laughing, and jumping for joy;
I'm singing your song, High God.
PSALM 9:2 MSG

Rejoice in the Lord always. I will say it again: Rejoice!
PHILIPPIANS 4:4 NIV

Daily Prayer . . . for wisdom

*If you need wisdom—if you want to know what
God wants you to do—ask him, and he will gladly tell you.
He will not resent your asking.*
JAMES 1:5–6 NLT

Dear Heavenly Father,

During all of my years spent getting an education, I've gained a lot of head knowledge. But all that I've learned won't do me any good if I don't have the ability to apply it to my real life. I need Your wisdom for that, Lord. My teachers were great, but You are the teacher I need as I put my knowledge to work.

Each day, I pray that You will guide me in making the right choices. Only You can help me lead a balanced life. Please show me how to keep my priorities straight and use what I've learned for Your glory.

Amen.

*Tune your ears to the world of Wisdom;
set your heart on a life of Understanding.*
PROVERBS 2:2 MSG

Learning sleeps and snores in libraries, but wisdom is everywhere, wide awake, on tiptoe.

Josh Billings

MY PERSONAL PRAYER

Dear Father:

_____

_____

_____

_____

_____

_____

_____

_____

Amen

We ask God to fill you with the knowledge of his will, with all the wisdom and understanding that his Spirit gives.
COLOSSIANS 1:9 GNT

Getting wisdom is the most important thing you can do!
PROVERBS 4:7 NLT

Daily Prayer . . . for self-control

Think clearly and exercise self-control.
Look forward to the special blessings that will come.
1 PETER 1:13 NLT

Dear Heavenly Father,

The world is a wild and chaotic place. There are so many choices to make now that I'm out of school—so many distractions to keep me from doing what I know I should. Please help me exercise self-control and keep my feet on the right path. We both know I can't do it on my own.

I ask You, Lord, to give me a sharp eye in spotting temptation and an obedient spirit that is strong and wise enough to say no at the right times. More than anything, I want my life to be pleasing to You. I want to reach the full potential You've placed in me. Thanks for helping me realize all You created me to be.

Amen.

The grace of God teaches us to say "No" to ungodliness
and worldly passions, and to live self-controlled,
upright and godly lives.
TITUS 2:11–12 NIV

He who reigns within himself and rules his passions, desires, and fears is more than a king.

John Milton

MY PERSONAL PRAYER

Dear Father:

_____

_____

_____

_____

_____

_____

_____

Amen

Learn to put aside your own desires so that you will become patient and godly, gladly letting God have his way with you.
2 PETER 1:6–7 TLB

All athletes practice strict self-control. They do it to win a prize that will fade away, but we do it for an eternal prize.
1 CORINTHIANS 9:25 NLT

Daily Prayer . . . for comfort

The God and Father of our Lord Jesus Christ . . . is the source of every mercy and the God who comforts us. He comforts us in all our troubles so that we can comfort others.
2 CORINTHIANS 1:3–4 NLT

Dear Heavenly Father,

I'm having a blue day—a sad day. I worked so hard to graduate and now that it's over, I miss my friends. I miss the routine and rhythm of campus life. I'm uneasy with the changes that are coming.

Please wrap Your strong, supporting arms around me, Lord. I need to hear Your words of love and comfort right now. Remind me of all the wonderful things You've placed in my life, the countless blessings You send my way. Replace my sadness with Your joy. Help me turn my face from the past and look to the future and what You are about to teach me.

Amen.

As a mother comforts her child, so I'll comfort you.
ISAIAH 66:13 MSG

If I can stop one heart from breaking, I shall not live in vain.

Emily Dickinson

MY PERSONAL PRAYER

Dear Father:

_____

_____

_____

_____

_____

_____

_____

_____

_____

Amen

The LORD is close to the brokenhearted.
PSALM 34:18 NLT

*You, O LORD, will increase my honor
and comfort me once again.*
PSALM 71:21 NIV

Daily Prayer . . . for forgiveness

If we admit our sins—make a clean breast of them—
he won't let us down; he'll be true to himself.
He'll forgive our sins and purge us of all wrongdoing.
1 JOHN 1:9 MSG

Dear Heavenly Father,

I've really blown it this time. I've hurt You and I've hurt myself with my thoughtless words and actions. I have no excuse. I know what I've done, and I'm sorry for it. I ask for Your grace and mercy as I kneel at Your feet.

Thank You for providing a way out for me, an opportunity for forgiveness even before I knew I needed it. Thank You for sending Your Son Jesus to cover all my sins with His precious blood. Wash me clean and help me get up from here a changed person—changed by Your grace (Your unmerited favor) and changed by Your love.

Amen.

Jesus said, "If you forgive others their trespasses,
your heavenly Father will also forgive you."
MATTHEW 6:14 NRSV

Nothing in this lost and ruined world bears the meek impress of the Son of God so surely as forgiveness.

Alice Cary

MY PERSONAL PRAYER

Dear Father:

_____

_____

_____

_____

_____

_____

_____

Amen

*Be kind to one another, tenderhearted, forgiving one another,
even as God in Christ forgave you.*
EPHESIANS 4:32

*By the sacrificial death of Christ we are set free, that is,
our sins are forgiven. How great is the grace of God!*
EPHESIANS 1:7–8 GNT

Daily Prayer . . . for protection

The LORD will keep you safe from all hidden dangers and from all deadly diseases. He will cover you with his wings; you will be safe in his care; his faithfulness will protect and defend you.
PSALM 91:3–4 GNT

Dear Heavenly Father,

While I was in school, I felt reasonably safe. The future seemed hypothetical. But that was then . . . this is now! Suddenly, life is kind of in my face. I'm aware of dangers I never took seriously before.

Lord, when I feel frightened and insecure, please hide me in the shelter of Your love. I trust in You to protect me. At school, I only imagined I was safe—with You I know I am. You see the future and know every single circumstance I will ever face. Nothing that happens to me will surprise You, and You will always be right at my side through thick and thin. Thanks, Lord!

Amen.

The LORD says, "I will rescue those who love me.
I will protect those who trust in my name."
PSALM 91:14 NLT

I will not fear, for You are ever with me, and You will never leave me to face my perils alone.

Thomas Merton

MY PERSONAL PRAYER

Dear Father:

_____

_____

_____

_____

_____

_____

_____

_____

Amen

The LORD will deliver me from every evil attack and
will bring me safely to his heavenly Kingdom.
2 TIMOTHY 4:18 NLT

You are a hiding place for me; you preserve me from trouble;
you surround me with glad cries of deliverance.
PSALM 32:7 NRSV

Daily Prayer . . . for courage

When they saw the courage of Peter and John and realized that they were unschooled, ordinary men, they were astonished and they took note that these men had been with Jesus.
ACTS 4:13 NIV

Dear Heavenly Father,

It was much easier to sit in a classroom and study other people's lives than it was to walk through those front doors and into the real world. Out here, theory ends and reality begins. It's so much more difficult to make choices for myself than it was to speculate on the decisions made by historical figures.

What I need from You, Lord, is courage—enough to face the challenges that lie ahead. Enough to honestly evaluate my own weaknesses so that I won't stumble over myself. Enough to keep my heart focused on Your will and purpose for my life. Infuse me with enough courage to become all that You created me to be.

Amen.

Be strong and courageous! The Lord your God will go ahead of you. He will neither fail you nor forsake you.
DEUTERONOMY 31:6 NLT

Courage is resistance to fear, mastery of fear, not absence of fear.

Mark Twain

MY PERSONAL PRAYER

Dear Father:

_____

_____

_____

_____

_____

_____

_____

_____

Amen

> GOD's now at my side and I'm not afraid;
> who would dare lay a hand on me?
> PSALM 118:6 MSG

> Be strong, vigorous, and of good courage.
> JOSHUA 1:18 AMP

Daily Prayer . . . for strength

The joy of the LORD is your strength.
NEHEMIAH 8:10 NIV

Dear Heavenly Father,

All that studying—all those exams. Long days and late nights were the norm when I was in school. But as I think back, a student's life seems easier than the one I'm facing now. Back then, I could make up an assignment, retake a missed test, collaborate with others. But real life is different. It's final. It's lonely. It feels so overwhelming at times.

When I'm feeling weak and vulnerable, Lord, You are the only one I can turn to for help. Strengthen me. Energize me. Fill me with Your power and might that I might stand tall and move forward and accomplish those things that You've placed in my heart.

Amen.

The LORD is my rock and my fortress and my deliverer;
my God, my strength, in whom I will trust.
PSALM 18:2

He knows not his own strength that hath not met adversity.

Ben Jonson

MY PERSONAL PRAYER

Dear Father:

_____

_____

_____

_____

_____

_____

_____

Amen

The LORD gives me power and strength; he is my savior.
ISAIAH 12:2 GNT

The LORD gives me honor; he is the source of my strength.
ISAIAH 49:5 GNT

Daily Prayer . . . for rest

If you sit down, you will not be afraid;
when you lie down, your sleep will be sweet.
PROVERBS 3:24 NRSV

Dear Heavenly Father,

I've been tired before—after a late night of cramming for an exam or finishing a term paper. But I've never experienced mental fatigue like this. So many changes. So many crucial decisions. When I close my eyes, my thoughts plow into one another, my mind racing from one question to another. Lord, I really need a good night's sleep, but beyond that, I need Your rest—mind, body, and spirit.

Please calm my mind. Bring peace to my thoughts. I lay all of my concerns at Your feet, asking You to help me make sense of everything. You are such a wonderful Father! Thank You for helping me find rest in You.

Amen.

The LORD said, "My Presence will go with you,
and I will give you rest."
EXODUS 33:14

Don't fight with the pillow, but lay down your head
And kick every worriment out of the bed.

Edmund Vance Cooke

MY PERSONAL PRAYER

Dear Father:

_____

_____

_____

_____

_____

_____

_____

_____

Amen

Be still and rest in the Lord.
PSALM 37:7 AMP

*Jesus said, "Come to me, all of you who are weary and
carry heavy burdens, and I will give you rest."*
MATTHEW 11:28 NLT

Daily Prayer . . . for hope

Without wavering, let us hold tightly to the hope we say we
have, for God can be trusted to keep his promise.
HEBREWS 10:23–24 NLT

Dear Heavenly Father,

While I was in school, I lived on a diet of hope—
hope that I would do well, finish my course of
study, find the perfect job. You faithfully saw me
through those days, Lord. When I thought
graduation day would never come, You picked me
up and renewed my expectations for the future.

Well, here I am at last. Graduation has come,
and once again, I place my hope in You for
tomorrow. Hope that I can make a difference in the
world around me, thinking more of others than of
myself. Without You, life would be pretty bleak, but
with You, I can look forward to the days ahead and
the life of adventure You have planned for me.

Amen.

With that kind of hope to excite us, nothing holds us back.
2 CORINTHIANS 3:12 MSG

In the face of uncertainty, there is nothing wrong with hope.

Bernie Siegel

MY PERSONAL PRAYER

Dear Father:

_____

_____

_____

_____

_____

_____

_____

Amen

No one whose hope is in you will ever be put to shame.
PSALM 25:3 NIV

*Be strong and let your heart take courage, all you who
wait for and hope for and expect the Lord!*
PSALM 31:24 AMP

Daily Prayer . . . for patience

May you be made strong . . . so that you may be able
to endure everything with patience.
COLOSSIANS 1:11 GNT

Dear Heavenly Father,

Give me patience—and give it to me now! It seems like all I do is wait: wait in line, wait at stoplights, wait for a phone call, wait for all the pieces of my post-graduation life to fall into place!

I need a double-dose of Your patience. Please stop my foot-tapping and help me learn to wait patiently for all the good things You have in store for me. Show me when to act and when to wait for Your timing. And thank You, Lord, for being so patient with me, even when I act impulsively, barreling past Your purposes. Thank You for loving me in spite of myself.

Amen.

Since God chose you to be the holy people whom he loves,
you must clothe yourselves with tenderhearted mercy,
kindness, humility, gentleness, and patience.
COLOSSIANS 3:12 NLT

Our patience will achieve more than our force.

Edmund Burke

MY PERSONAL PRAYER

Dear Father:

_____

_____

_____

_____

_____

_____

_____

Amen

A man's wisdom gives him patience.
PROVERBS 19:11 NIV

Be patient. Stay steady and strong.
JAMES 5:8 MSG

Daily Prayer . . . for contentment

There is great gain in godliness combined with contentment.
1 TIMOTHY 6:6–7 NRSV

Dear Heavenly Father,

I've waited so long and worked so hard to finish school. Now my mind races with thoughts of a big salary, lots of possessions, position and status. All that I've ever wanted feels like it's finally within reach. It's kind of fun imagining what my life will be like.

But, Lord, I don't want to get caught up in materialism, thinking more about grown-up toys than of who I really am—Your child. Please help me to keep my life in balance, my priorities straight, and my eyes focused on You. Thank You for Your contentment in my life.

Amen.

If God gives a man wealth and property and lets him enjoy them, he should be grateful and enjoy what he has worked for. It is a gift from God.
ECCLESIASTES 5:19 GNT

I am always content with what happens; for I know that what God chooses is better than what I choose.

Epictetus

MY PERSONAL PRAYER

Dear Father:

_____

_____

_____

_____

_____

_____

_____

_____

Amen

I have learned the secret of contentment in every situation, whether it be a full stomach or hunger, plenty or want.
PHILIPPIANS 4:12 TLB

The fear of the LORD leads to life: then one rests content, untouched by trouble.
PROVERBS 19:23 NIV

Daily Prayer . . . for perseverance

Let us run with perseverance the race that is set before us,
looking to Jesus the pioneer and perfecter of our faith.
HEBREWS 12:1–2 NRSV

Dear Heavenly Father,

The great thing about school is that it's broken up into semesters. I worked really hard, but I always knew that at the end of the term, I'd get a break. There would be time to play. But I can already see that life after graduation isn't like that. It's like a marathon, and I'm already exhausted and want to give up.

Teach me to persevere, Lord, and to look to You for strength and energy when my own has been used up. Remind me that You are all I need to make it through each day. I want to stay on course, putting my trust in You, until I've accomplished all that You have for me.

Amen.

Blessed is the man who perseveres under trial, because when
he has stood the test, he will receive the crown of life.
JAMES 1:12 NIV

By perseverance, the snail reached the ark.

Charles Spurgeon

MY PERSONAL PRAYER

Dear Father:

_____

_____

_____

_____

_____

_____

_____

_____

Amen

I strain to reach the end of the race and receive the prize
for which God is calling us up to heaven.
PHILIPPIANS 3:14 TLB

To those who by persistence in doing good seek glory,
honor and immortality, God will give eternal life.
ROMANS 2:7 NIV

Daily Prayer . . . for purpose

*It is in Christ that we find out who we are
and what we are living for.*
EPHESIANS 1:11 MSG

Dear Heavenly Father,

While I was in school, I thought I had all the answers. I thought I had my future all mapped out. With all the required courses under my belt, I tackled my major. Graduation waited at the end like a shining victory.

But now things don't seem so clear. There are even more difficult questions to answer, especially at this time in my life when everything is changing so quickly. Why was I created? What am I here for? What should I do with my life? Are my plans consistent with Your purpose?

Show me the way, Lord. Help me to find Your purpose for my life because I know it's the only path to success.

Amen.

*Everything, absolutely everything, above and below,
visible and invisible . . . everything got started in him
and finds its purpose in him.*
COLOSSIANS 1:16 MSG

The man without a purpose is like a ship without a rudder—a waif, a nothing, a no man.

Thomas Carlyle

MY PERSONAL PRAYER

Dear Father:

_____

_____

_____

_____

_____

_____

_____

_____

Amen

God has made us what we are, and in our union with Christ Jesus he has created us for a life of good deeds, which he has already prepared for us to do.
EPHESIANS 2:10 GNT

You, LORD, give perfect peace to those who keep their purpose firm and put their trust in you.
ISAIAH 26:3 GNT

Daily Prayer . . . for my parents

Honor (esteem and value as precious) your father and your mother—this is the first commandment with a promise.
EPHESIANS 6:2 AMP

Dear Heavenly Father,

As I grow older, I realize more and more what a blessing my parents were to me while I was in school. Even though I haven't always agreed with their viewpoint, I'm so grateful that You placed them in my life to guide and train me. I can't imagine what it would have been like without their example.

Lord, help me to remember and put into practice all the things my parents taught me. As I mature and move forward, remind me to always respect, honor, and cherish them for who they are and what they have meant to me, even when we disagree.

Amen.

Children, obey your parents because you belong to the Lord, for this is the right thing to do.
EPHESIANS 6:1 NLT

Lucky parents who have fine children usually have lucky children who have fine parents.

James A. Brewer

MY PERSONAL PRAYER

Dear Father:

_____

_____

_____

_____

_____

_____

_____

_____

Amen

Pay attention to what your father and mother tell you.
Their teaching will improve your character.
PROVERBS 1:8–9 GNT

Listen to your father, who gave you life, and don't despise
your mother's experience when she is old.
PROVERBS 23:22 NLT

Daily Prayer . . . for my siblings

How wonderful it is, how pleasant,
when brothers live together in harmony!
PSALM 133:1 NLT

Dear Heavenly Father,

What great times I've had with my brothers and sisters! Thank You so much for allowing me to grow up in a family that was full of fun and pranks, fights and quarrels, sharing and laughter, and lots of love. I've noticed that things are changing though as we graduate and go our separate ways. It would be easy to let time and distance come between us.

Lord, help me to take the lead with my brothers and sisters, keeping them close, loving and encouraging them. No matter where Your plan for my life takes me, remind me to pray for them every day.

Amen.

Strengthen and build up the faith of your brothers.
LUKE 2:32 TLB

I think, am sure, a brother's love exceeds all the world's love in its unworldliness.

Robert Browning

MY PERSONAL PRAYER

Dear Father:

_____

_____

_____

_____

_____

_____

_____

Amen

Jesus replied, "My mother and my brothers are all those who hear the message of God and obey it."
LUKE 8:21 NLT

Be devoted to one another in brotherly love; give preference to one another in honor.
ROMANS 12:10–11 NASB

Daily Prayer . . . for my relatives

Ruth replied, "I will go wherever you go and live wherever you live. Your people will be my people, and your God will be my God."
RUTH 1:16-17 NLT

Dear Heavenly Father,

Thank You for my relatives. I know You had a purpose in choosing this family for me, and I ask that You fulfill that purpose in all of our lives, especially now as I enter the real world after graduation. Lord, there are so many of my relations who still need to know You. Please make Yourself real to them—so real that they can't help but see You for who You really are, our Savior and Lord.

They all need Your help, Your joy, Your peace, and Your comfort today. Be near to them in the way they need it most. Teach me to be sensitive to their needs, and show me how to love and encourage them.

Amen.

They answered, "Believe in the Lord Jesus, and you will be saved—you and your family."
ACTS 16:31 GNT

A happy family is but an earlier heaven.

Sir John Browning

MY PERSONAL PRAYER

Dear Father:

_____

_____

_____

_____

_____

_____

_____

Amen

You are members of God's family.
EPHESIANS 2:19 NLT

*Give clothes to those who need them, and do not hide
from relatives who need your help.*
ISAIAH 58:7 NLT

Daily Prayer . . . for my best friend

Friend, you have no idea how good your love makes me feel.
PHILEMON 17 MSG

Dear Heavenly Father,

It's so cool to have a best friend who "gets" me! We have so much fun together, telling stories, hanging out, and sharing secrets. Lord, besides You, my best friend knows more about me than anyone else. As I move into a new phase of life after graduation, all the great memories we've made over the years have become even more special to me.

Thank You for this awesome gift of friendship. As the years go by, please help my friend and I to grow even closer. No matter what life brings our way, remind us to always be honest and draw near to each other and to You.

Amen.

As iron sharpens iron, a friend sharpens a friend.
PROVERBS 27:17 NLT

There is nothing on this earth more to be prized than true friendship.

Saint Thomas Aquinas

MY PERSONAL PRAYER

Dear Father:

_____

_____

_____

_____

_____

_____

_____

_____

Amen

*Dear friend, I pray that you may enjoy good health
and that all may go well with you, even as your soul
is getting along well.*
3 JOHN 1:2 NIV

A friend means well, even when he hurts you.
PROVERBS 27:6 GNT

Daily Prayer . . . for my friendships

One standing alone can be attacked and defeated,
but two can stand back-to-back and conquer; three is
even better, for a triple-braided cord is not easily broken.
ECCLESIASTES 4:12 TLB

Dear Heavenly Father,

When I look at my life at this point, I can see that I have been truly blessed—not with cars, jewelry, or stereo equipment, but with what really matters: true friendships. My friends have stuck with me through thick and thin—through late-night study sessions to pizza parties and movies, right up to the day we walked across the stage to receive our diplomas!

As life continues, Lord, please bless my friends in the ways they need it most. Help us to remain friends, to be there for each other when times are tough, and to rejoice together when good things happen. Thank You so much for the amazing gift of friendship!

Amen.

A man that hath friends must shew himself friendly.
PROVERBS 18:24 KJV

If you want an accounting of your worth, count your friends.

Merry Browne

MY PERSONAL PRAYER

Dear Father:

_____

_____

_____

_____

_____

_____

_____

_____

Amen

Friends always show their love.
What are brothers for if not to share trouble?
PROVERBS 17:17 GNT

If one person falls, the other can reach out and help.
But people who are alone when they fall are in real trouble.
ECCLESIASTES 4:10 NLT

Daily Prayer . . . for my future spouse

*A man leaves his father and his mother
and clings to his wife, and they become one flesh.*
GENESIS 2:24 NRSV

Dear Heavenly Father,
 Since my childhood, I've dreamed about getting married and who my future spouse might be. I know that marriage is a good thing, designed by You to bless Your people. Someday You will bring the right person into my life—the one You have chosen just for me. Help me to be patient and not jump the gun with the wrong person.
 Bless my future spouse right now. Until the day we finally meet, help us both to grow in strength and maturity—to resist temptation, to make the right decisions, and to cultivate more than outward attractiveness. Develop our characters as we follow You.
 Amen.

*The man who finds a wife finds a good thing;
she is a blessing to him from the Lord.*
PROVERBS 18:22 TLB

Love built on beauty, soon as beauty, dies.

John Donne

MY PERSONAL PRAYER

Dear Father:

_____

_____

_____

_____

_____

_____

_____

_____

Amen

A wise, understanding, and prudent wife is from the Lord.
PROVERBS 19:14 AMP

How beautiful you are, my love; how your eyes shine with love!
How handsome you are, my dearest; how you delight me!
SONG OF SONGS 1:15–16 GNT

Daily Prayer . . . for my enemies

*We are not fighting against human beings but against
the wicked spiritual forces in the heavenly world.*
EPHESIANS 6:12 GNT

Dear Heavenly Father,

There are former students I just can't get along with, no matter how hard I try. You know who they are—the snide, cruel ones, who always tried to make me look bad and couldn't stand to see me succeed. It's hard to pray for my enemies, Lord, but I know that Your desire is for me to live in peace with them.

Many of them I'll never see again after graduation, but their actions will always be a part of my school memories. Teach me to love them in the same way You loved those who abused You and arranged Your death. You know I can't do it without You, Lord. Thank You for the power to bless my enemies.

Amen.

Love your enemies and pray for those who persecute you.
MATTHEW 5:44 NASB

It pays to know the enemy—not least because at some time you may have the opportunity to turn him into a friend.

Margaret Thatcher

MY PERSONAL PRAYER

Dear Father:

_____

_____

_____

_____

_____

_____

_____

_____

Amen

Jesus said, "Do not resist an evildoer. But if anyone strikes you on the right cheek, turn the other also."
MATTHEW 5:39 NRSV

When the ways of people please the Lord, he causes even their enemies to be at peace with them.
PROVERBS 16:7 NRSV

Daily Prayer . . . for my school

Jesus said, "A student is not greater than the teacher. But the student who works hard will become like the teacher."
LUKE 6:40 NLT

Dear Heavenly Father,

Many times over the past years I've looked ahead and wondered if the day would really come when I would turn in the last assignment and take the last exam. But it's happened—finally! As I look back at this special time in my life, I'm so grateful for the teachers, mentors, and even other students who have poured themselves into my life so that I could prepare for the road ahead of me.

Lord, please continue to bless my school, even as I leave it behind. Thank You that not only is my pail filled with knowledge, but my fire has also been lit to continue on a lifetime pursuit of learning.

Amen.

God gave these four young men an unusual aptitude for learning the literature and science of the time.
DANIEL 1:17 NLT

Education is not the filling of a pail, but the lighting of a fire.

William Butler Yeats

MY PERSONAL PRAYER

Dear Father:

_____

_____

_____

_____

_____

_____

_____

Amen

Under Gamaliel I was thoroughly trained in the law of our fathers and was just as zealous for God as any of you are today.
ACTS 22:3 NIV

I ponder every morsel of wisdom from you, I attentively watch how you've done it. I relish everything you've told me of life, I won't forget a word of it.
PSALM 119:15–16 MSG

Daily Prayer . . . for my boss

*Work with a smile on your face, always keeping in mind
that no matter who happens to be giving the orders,
you're really serving God.*
EPHESIANS 6:7 MSG

Dear Heavenly Father,

Work is not always fun, especially now when my career is just getting started and I'm at the bottom of the chain of command. But I realize that coming under authority is part of Your plan for me. Show me how to please my boss, whether I like my job duties or not, and help me to see that in honoring my boss, I am honoring You.

Teach me to be respectful and cheerful at all times—not just when I feel like it. Remind me always to reflect Your grace in my life and show my boss that I'm a dependable person and someone committed to bringing excellence to my job.

Amen.

*Obey your earthly masters in everything you do. Try to
please them all the time, not just when they are watching you.
Obey them willingly because of your reverent fear of the Lord.*
COLOSSIANS 3:22 NLT

It's easy to make a buck. It's a lot tougher to make a difference.

Tom Brokaw

MY PERSONAL PRAYER

Dear Father:

_____

_____

_____

_____

_____

_____

_____

_____

Amen

Do everything readily and cheerfully—
no bickering, no second-guessing allowed!
PHILIPPIANS 2:14 MSG

Work hard and cheerfully at whatever you do, as though
you were working for the Lord rather than for people.
COLOSSIANS 3:23 NLT

Daily Prayer . . . for my co-workers

We want to work together with you so you will be full of joy.
2 CORINTHIANS 1:24 NLT

Dear Heavenly Father,

As a new graduate, I'm so grateful for my career and for the people I work with. Thank You for making me part of a team that can pull together to get the job done. But I know that the lives of my co-workers extend far beyond the workplace. Please help me to notice when one of them is troubled or when another might need someone to listen, to laugh with, or to talk to as a friend.

Lord, some of my co-workers don't know You, and so I ask You to help me be an effective witness of Your love to them. Most of all, let me be a blessing in the lives of my co-workers—for Your glory.

Amen.

I want to work among you and see good results.
ROMANS 1:13 NLT

No matter what accomplishments you achieve, somebody helps you.

Althea Gibson

MY PERSONAL PRAYER

Dear Father:

_____

_____

_____

_____

_____

_____

_____

_____

Amen

When the sun comes up . . . men and women go out to work,
busy at their jobs until evening.
PSALM 104:22–23 MSG

Each one of us does the work which the Lord gave him to do.
1 CORINTHIANS 3:5 GNT

Daily Prayer . . . for my church

When they said, "Let's go to the house of God,"
my heart leaped for joy.
PSALM 122:1 MSG

Dear Heavenly Father,

I love my church family! During my school years, my friends in youth group were always there for me, whether I needed a shoulder to cry on, someone to pray with, or a friend to laugh with. It's so wonderful to meet together with other Christians to worship You and help each other through good and bad times.

It's amazing to think of the church as Your body, moving as Your hands and feet and voice in the earth. Knowing I'm a part of Your work is an incredible privilege! Thank You for using us in our community to share Your love with others, and thanks for all You are doing as we assemble together.

Amen.

The church is his body; it is filled by Christ,
who fills everything everywhere with his presence.
EPHESIANS 5:23 NLT

The Church after all is not a club of saints; it is a hospital for sinners.

George Craig Stewart

MY PERSONAL PRAYER

Dear Father:

_____

_____

_____

_____

_____

_____

_____

Amen

Let us not neglect our church meetings, as some people do,
but encourage and warn each other, especially now that the
day of his coming back again is drawing near.
HEBREWS 10:25 TLB

Christ's love makes the church whole. His words
evoke her beauty. Everything he does and says
is designed to bring out the best in her.
EPHESIANS 5:27 MSG

Daily Prayer . . . for those in need

All eyes look to you for help, O LORD; you give them their food as they need it. When you open your hand, you satisfy the hunger and thirst of every living thing.
PSALM 145:15–16 NLT

Dear Heavenly Father,

No matter where I turn, I see people in need—on street corners, in restaurants, at the grocery store, and even on the television news at night. People everywhere struggle just to feed their children. I'm so blessed with clothes to wear, food to eat, a comfortable bed to sleep in each night, and a bright and promising future now that I've graduated.

Father, I know You care no less for any one of them than You care for me. Show me real, practical ways to help. Don't let me pass by a person in need without demonstrating Your love and concern.

Amen.

Real religion, the kind that passes muster before God the Father, is this: Reach out to the homeless and loveless in their plight.
JAMES 1:27 MSG

Great opportunities to help others seldom come, but small ones surround us every day.

Sally Koch

MY PERSONAL PRAYER

Dear Father:

_____

_____

_____

_____

_____

_____

_____

_____

Amen

When God's children are in need,
you be the one to help them out.
ROMANS 12:13 TLB

Jesus said, "Sell what you have and give to those in need.
This will store up treasure for you in heaven!"
LUKE 12:33 NLT

Daily Prayer . . . for our country

Blessed is the nation whose God is the Lord.
PSALM 33:12 NASB

Dear Heavenly Father,

What a great country we live in, where I was able to freely attend school and graduate! I'm so proud of our nation and everything You have accomplished through her in this world. Please keep our country strong, able to stand against all of our enemies—both at home and abroad. Even more than military strength, Lord, I ask You to return our country to its devotion to You and the principles of Your Word.

Please give the leaders of our country the wisdom they need to make sound decisions, and help me be a ready to do my part, regardless of whether that part is small or great.

Amen.

Make the Master proud of you by being good citizens.
Respect the authorities, whatever their level; they are
God's emissaries for keeping order.
1 PETER 2:13–14 MSG

A country free enough to examine its own conscience is a land worth living in, a nation to be envied.

Prince Charles

MY PERSONAL PRAYER

Dear Father:

_____

_____

_____

_____

_____

_____

_____

Amen

God-devotion makes a country strong.
PROVERBS 14:34 MSG

*Let me see the prosperity of your people
and share in the happiness of your nation.*
PSALM 106:5 GNT

Daily Prayer . . . for the world

God claims Earth and everything in it;
God claims World and all who live on it.
PSALM 24:1 MSG

Dear Heavenly Father,

You have created such a big, fascinating world, full of amazing people, cultures, and nations. Now that I've graduated, I can't wait to experience what You have planned for me out there!

I know that You love every person on the earth just as much as You love me, Lord, and Your heart is grieved when war, terrorism, famine, natural disasters, and disease wreak havoc and interrupt Your plans for them.

Bring peace to Your creation, Father. Turn the hearts of people everywhere back to You. Help me to be a part of telling the world about Your great love and spreading the Good News of Your Son Jesus to every corner of the globe.

Amen.

Give thanks to the Lord and proclaim his greatness.
Let the whole world know what he has done.
PSALM 105:1 NLT

Your love has a broken wing if it cannot fly across the sea.
Malthie D. Babcock

MY PERSONAL PRAYER

Dear Father:

_____

_____

_____

_____

_____

_____

_____

_____

Amen

Peoples from the remotest lands will worship him.
PSALM 67:7 TLB

*In every nation whoever fears Him
and works righteousness is accepted by Him.*
ACTS 10:35

Daily Prayer . . . for my future

*God says: "I know what I'm doing. I have it all
planned out—plans to take care of you, not abandon you,
plans to give you the future you hope for."*
JEREMIAH 29:11 MSG

Dear Heavenly Father,

What will my life be like this time next year? In five years? In ten? So many changes are taking place after graduation, and I hope I'm making the right choices. You've placed so many hopes and dreams in my heart, and I want to get started on everything right away. Give me wisdom, though, to wait for Your green light.

You know better than I do what lies ahead. Help me trust in Your great plan for my life, and when I make a mistake, please work everything together for my good. Show me Your will, and I will follow it, because I know that trusting You will bring a future more wonderful than I can imagine.

Amen.

My future is in your hands, O Lord.
PSALM 31:15 NLT

Anticipating is even more fun than recollecting.

Malcolm S. Forbes

MY PERSONAL PRAYER

Dear Father:

_____

_____

_____

_____

_____

_____

_____

_____

Amen

Soak yourself in the Fear-of-God—that's where your future lies.
PROVERBS 23:17–18 MSG

*Look at those who are honest and good, for a wonderful
future lies before those who love peace.*
PSALM 37:37 NLT

I cried aloud in midnight gloom,
With pleading word;
I spoke of sorrow's threat'ning doom,
Of hope deferred;
And lo, God heard my anguished cry—
And e'en my lowest, faintest sigh!

Henry W. Frost

Daily Prayers for Help . . .

Daily Prayer for help . . . when I'm feeling unloved

I'll call nobodies and make them somebodies;
I'll call the unloved and make them beloved.
ROMANS 9:25 MSG

Dear Heavenly Father,

Maybe it's the letdown after graduation, but some days I wake up feeling like the most worthless, unlovable person in town. Sometimes it's caused by someone's remark or slight, but often, it's just there, like a monster lurking under the bed. When days like that come along, help me to fight back with what I know to be true.

Remind me that You created me, that I am unique among all of Your children, that You loved me even before I was born, and that I'm priceless in Your sight. Please wrap Your arms around me, Lord, and embrace me with Your love.

Amen.

The LORD lavishes his love on those who love him
and obey his commands.
DEUTERONOMY 5:10 NLT

God doesn't love us because we are special—we are special because God loves us!

William Arthur Ward

MY PERSONAL PRAYER

Dear Father:

_____

_____

_____

_____

_____

_____

_____

Amen

God says, "I've never quit loving you and never will.
Expect love, love, and more love!"
JEREMIAH 31:3 MSG

See how very much our heavenly Father loves us, for he
allows us to be called his children, and we really are!
1 JOHN 3:1 NLT

Daily Prayer for help . . . when I'm struggling with peer pressure

Dear friend, if bad companions tempt you,
don't go along with them.
PROVERBS 1:10 MSG

Dear Heavenly Father,

"Come party with us! Let's have a good time!" That's what certain people have been saying to me lately—that and other things to get me to act in ways I know I shouldn't. I thought growing up and graduating would put an end to all that peer pressure, but it looks like I've just changed peer groups. If anything, the pressures seem stronger and more compelling.

I want to live a life pleasing to You, Lord. Give me the courage of my convictions, so I will only do those things that I know to be right and good, regardless of what anyone thinks or what everyone else is doing. Thank You, Lord, for Your strength today.

Amen.

Jesus said, "God blesses you who are hated and excluded and
mocked and cursed because you are identified with me."
LUKE 6:22 NLT

Character is much easier kept than recovered.

Thomas Paine

MY PERSONAL PRAYER

Dear Father:

_____

_____

_____

_____

_____

_____

_____

Amen

The righteous should choose his friends carefully.
PROVERBS 12:26

An honorable person stands firm for what is right.
ISAIAH 32:8 GNT

Daily Prayer for help . . . when I'm disappointed

The Scriptures tell us, "Anyone who believes in God will not be disappointed."
ROMANS 10:11 NLT

Dear Heavenly Father,

Disappointment hurts! I got my hopes up, and things didn't quite work out the way I thought they would . . . again. When will I learn to see events from Your perspective, Lord? You see the big picture, but it's harder for me.

Now that graduation is over, You know what's next in Your plan for my life. So I'm here, Lord, to let You know I trust You even when I can't see what's around the next curve. I hand over my disappointment and ask You to give me renewed hope in its place. Show me how to get back on track and stir up a new flame in my heart for the next challenge.

Amen.

O Lord, our ancestors called to you and escaped from danger; they trusted you and were not disappointed.
PSALM 22:5 GNT

We must accept finite disappointment, but we must never lose infinite hope.

Martin Luther King, Jr.

MY PERSONAL PRAYER

Dear Father:

_____

_____

_____

_____

_____

_____

_____

Amen

The vision is yet for an appointed time and it hastens to the end [fulfillment]; it will not deceive or disappoint.
HABAKKUK 2:3 AMP

This hope in God does not disappoint us, for God has poured out his love into our hearts by means of the Holy Spirit.
ROMANS 5:5 GNT

Daily Prayer for help . . . when I'm having problems at home

Let family members learn that religion begins at their own doorstep and that they should pay back with gratitude some of what they have received.
1 TIMOTHY 5:4 MSG

Dear Heavenly Father,

Since graduation, I'm not at home as much as I used to be, but it still hurts to know that it's a battleground on many days. My family's problems still weigh heavily on my mind and heart, and I can't seem to stop worrying about them. Lord, show me how to be a peacemaker, doing my part to bring unity to my parents and siblings and other close relations.

I pray for each member of my family and each of the relationships that make up our unique family group. Work with each person to surrender bitterness and resentment, selfishness and anger, and that includes me.

Amen.

Those who bring trouble on their families inherit only the wind.
PROVERBS 11:29 NLT

When home is ruled according to God's Word, angels might be asked to stay with us, and they would not find themselves out of their element.

Charles Spurgeon

MY PERSONAL PRAYER

Dear Father:

_____
_____
_____
_____
_____
_____
_____
_____

Amen

Jesus said, "Go home to your family and tell them how much the Lord has done for you, and how he has had mercy on you."
MARK 5:19 NIV

You are the light of the world—like a city on a mountain, glowing in the night for all to see. Don't hide your light under a basket! Instead, put it on a stand and let it shine for all.
MATTHEW 5:14–15 NLT

Daily Prayer for help . . . when I'm depressed

You, O LORD, will restore my life again; from the depths of the earth you will again bring me up.
PSALM 71:20 NIV

Dear Heavenly Father,

I've been so depressed since graduation, and I can't seem to pull myself up out of this dark pit. Who am I to think I'll ever accomplish anything great in life? Are You here with me in this horrible place? It's hard to feel You, but I know that You are there, regardless of what my thoughts are telling me.

Speak to my troubled mind, Lord, and chase away the clouds of despair. Because I trust in You, I gladly hand over all of my worries and cares. I set my heart on You and Your unchanging love to see me through this despondency. When You are all I have, You are enough.

Amen.

The burdens laid upon us were so great and so heavy that we gave up all hope of staying alive. But this happened so that we should rely, not on ourselves, but only on God. We have placed our hope in him that he will save us again.
2 CORINTHIANS 1:8–11 GNT

The happiness of your life depends upon the quality of your thoughts.

Marcus Antonius

MY PERSONAL PRAYER

Dear Father:

_____

_____

_____

_____

_____

_____

_____

Amen

GOD, rescue me, don't let me go under for good.
Let me see your great mercy full-face.
PSALM 69:14, 16 MSG

I still dare to hope when I remember this:
The unfailing love of the LORD never ends!
LAMENTATIONS 3:22 NLT

Daily Prayer for help . . . when I'm lonely

*God gives the lonely a home to live in
and leads prisoners out into happy freedom.*
PSALM 68:6 GNT

Dear Heavenly Father,

Since leaving school, even those I've called my friends have abandoned me, and there seems to be no one left who really cares. I've been left out, and I'm feeling all alone. I wish I had someone to talk to, to spend time with—someone who would love me for who I really am.

You are here, Lord. I know that for a fact. Thank You for being close to me during this time. As I learn to lean on You for everything I need, including friendship, teach me how to be a good friend. I know that when I reach out to others, my own loneliness will disappear, and the light of Your love will shine through my life.

Amen.

*Turn to me, LORD, and be merciful to me,
because I am lonely and weak.*
PSALM 25:16 GNT

Closer is He than breathing, and nearer than hands and feet.

Alfred, Lord Tennyson

MY PERSONAL PRAYER

Dear Father:

_____

_____

_____

_____

_____

_____

_____

_____

Amen

Jesus said, "I'll be with you, day after day after day, right up to the end of the age."
MATTHEW 28:20 MSG

The first time I was brought before the judge, no one was with me. Everyone had abandoned me. But the Lord stood with me and gave me strength.
2 TIMOTHY 4:16–17 NLT

Daily Prayer for help . . . when I've been rejected

He was despised and rejected—a man of sorrows,
acquainted with bitterest grief.
ISAIAH 53:3 NLT

Dear Heavenly Father,

I just don't understand. Before graduation, I assumed I was one of the "in" crowd—special—but I was wrong. Some "friends" have hurt me deeply because they decided I wasn't good enough. What's so wrong with me that I would be cast off like this? Lord, I know that You were abandoned, too. Please comfort my heart and make it clear to me that I am chosen and special in Your eyes.

Even when others reject me, Father, I know that You stand ready to take me in. I don't want to hold resentment in my heart, so I give this pain to You. Because I am chosen by You, I can face any situation with grace and dignity.

Amen.

Don't throw me out, don't abandon me; you've always
kept the door open. My father and mother walked out
and left me, but God took me in.
PSALM 27:9–10 MSG

It is the wounded oyster that mends its shell with pearl.

Ralph Waldo Emerson

MY PERSONAL PRAYER

Dear Father:

_____

_____

_____

_____

_____

_____

_____

Amen

God has not rejected his people.
ROMANS 11:2 GNT

*Jesus said, "When you are reviled and persecuted and
lied about because you are my followers—wonderful!
Be happy about it! Be very glad! for a tremendous
reward awaits you up in heaven."*
MATTHEW 5:11–12 TLB

Daily Prayer for help . . . when I'm physically ill

Whatever their illness and pain, or if they were possessed by demons, or were epileptics, or were paralyzed—Jesus healed them all.
MATTHEW 4:24 NLT

Dear Heavenly Father,

I feel lousy. I hate being sick, especially when it keeps me from doing the things I know You have for me to do. When I was in school, someone would write an excuse for me when I stayed home, but now I need to carry my weight at work. Whatever's wrong with me, Lord, please fix it. I know You want to see me back on my feet again.

Until that time, please help me to be patient. Give my doctor the wisdom to know what's wrong, and let the medicine that I take do its perfect work in my body. Thank You for the healing You purchased for me on the cross.

Amen.

By his wounds you have been healed.
1 PETER 2:24 NRSV

Prayer is not overcoming God's reluctance; it is laying hold of His highest willingness.

Richard Chenevix Trench

MY PERSONAL PRAYER

Dear Father:

_____

_____

_____

_____

_____

_____

_____

Amen

_This prayer made in faith will heal the sick person;
the Lord will restore him to health._
JAMES 5:15 GNT

I am the LORD, who heals you.
EXODUS 15:26 NRSV

Daily Prayer for help . . . when I'm fearful

*Say to those who are afraid, "Be strong,
and do not fear, for your God is coming to save you."*
ISAIAH 35:4 NLT

Dear Heavenly Father,

Now that I've graduated, life has become a much scarier place. In addition to crime, terrorist strikes, disease, and war, I'm afraid of my future and what will happen next. If I think about it too long, I could trigger a panic attack! It's so easy to be anxious when I don't keep my mind focused on You.

That's why You've told me, "Don't panic!" I know that because You're with me, everything will be all right. No matter what life brings my way, I can face it head on. You always give me the grace and the strength I need—right when I need it! Thank You for calming my fears.

Amen.

*"Don't panic. I'm with you.
There's no need to fear for I'm your God."*
ISAIAH 41:10 MSG

Courage is being scared to death—and saddling up anyway.
John Wayne

MY PERSONAL PRAYER

Dear Father:

_____

_____

_____

_____

_____

_____

_____

Amen

*Do not be afraid of those who kill the body but
cannot kill the soul; rather be afraid of God, who
can destroy both body and soul in hell.*
MATTHEW 10:28 GNT

*"Don't ever be afraid or discouraged," Joshua told his men.
"Be strong and courageous."*
JOSHUA 10:25 NLT

Daily Prayer for help . . . when I'm struggling with my appearance

The LORD doesn't make decisions the way you do!
People judge by outward appearance, but the Lord
looks at a person's thoughts and intentions.
1 SAMUEL 16:7 NLT

Dear Heavenly Father,

Why is it that everyone else seems so much more attractive than me? When I look in the mirror, I really don't like what I see—especially on a bad-hair day when I have an important job interview scheduled.

I'm not sure why You've made me the way I am, but I am making a decision today to see myself the way You see me. When I do beautiful things, I am beautiful, and when I act out of Christ's love and with His joy, people will naturally be attracted to me. The Holy Spirit living on the inside of me has transformed my imperfect body into a temple of God's beauty! Thank You, Lord.

Amen.

I want women to get in there with the men in humility
before God, not primping before a mirror or chasing
the latest fashions but doing something beautiful for God
and becoming beautiful doing it.
1 TIMOTHY 2:9–10 MSG

The kind of beauty I want most is the hard-to-get kind that comes from within—strength, courage, dignity.

Ruby Dee

MY PERSONAL PRAYER

Dear Father:

_____

_____

_____

_____

_____

_____

_____

_____

Amen

Do you not know that your body is a temple of
the Holy Spirit within you, which you have from God?
1 CORINTHIANS 6:19 NRSV

What matters is not your outer appearance—
but your inner disposition. Cultivate inner beauty,
the gentle, gracious kind God delights in.
1 PETER 3:3–4 MSG

Daily Prayer for help . . . when I'm discouraged

LORD, I weep with grief; my heart is heavy with sorrow; encourage and cheer me with your words.
PSALM 119:28 TLB

Dear Heavenly Father,

When things don't work out the way I want them to, when I get turned down for an interview, or a job, or even for a date, it's easy to get down in the dumps. It's so difficult to stay positive and upbeat about life's inevitable setbacks.

I don't want to be a person who caves in to despair every time something discouraging happens to me. Instead, I want to stand strong in You, unwavering, knowing that You ultimately work everything out for my good. No matter what might go wrong, You can make it right. Encourage me, Lord, to press on in life and stand strong in my faith. Amen.

When I pray, O LORD, you answer me; you encourage me by giving me the strength I need.
PSALM 138:3 NLT

You can measure a man by the opposition it takes to discourage him.

Robert C. Savage

MY PERSONAL PRAYER

Dear Father:

_____

_____

_____

_____

_____

_____

_____

Amen

As we have received mercy, we do not lose heart.
2 CORINTHIANS 4:1

*My purpose is to encourage you and assure you that
the grace of God is with you no matter what happens.*
1 PETER 5:12 NLT

Daily Prayer for help . . . when I'm worried

"Martha, Martha," the Lord answered, "you are worried and upset about many things, but only one thing is needed. Mary has chosen what is better, and it will not be taken away from her."
LUKE 10:41–42 NIV

Dear Heavenly Father,

What's going to happen now that I'm out of school? What if something goes wrong? What if I fail? What if it doesn't work out? What if? What if? What if? Father, my thoughts can drive me crazy if I let them. But worrying about things that might or might not happen just demonstrates that I haven't put my faith and trust completely in You.

I know that worry is a waste of time. So I choose to stop it right now and concentrate on what You are doing in my life today. When I begin to focus on the "now," I forget about tomorrow's "what ifs." Thank You for this new set of eyes that makes my worries disappear.

Amen.

Worry weighs a person down;
an encouraging word cheers a person up.
PROVERBS 12:25 NLT

The more you worry about other people's welfare, the less you will worry about your own.

Alvin E. Magary

MY PERSONAL PRAYER

Dear Father:

_____

_____

_____

_____

_____

_____

_____

Amen

*Give your entire attention to what God is doing right now,
and don't get worked up about what may or may not
happen tomorrow. God will help you deal with
whatever hard things come up when the time comes.*
MATTHEW 6:34 MSG

*Don't be afraid and don't worry. Instead,
you must worship Christ as Lord of your life.*
1 PETER 3:14–15 NLT

Daily Prayer for help . . . when I long to be married

When you're unmarried, you're free to concentrate on simply pleasing the Master.
1 CORINTHIANS 7:32 MSG

Dear Heavenly Father,

"Always a bridesmaid, never a bride," or, "Always a groomsman, but never the groom," people say jokingly. But what if it's true? Father, You know the deepest desires of my heart. You created marriage and called it "very good," so why is it taking so long to happen for me?

I really need Your patience—and Your guidance—in this area of my life. It would be so easy to choose the wrong person just to get married, but I want to wait for Your perfect will to be done in my life. As I'm waiting, build in me the character traits necessary for me to be a good spouse, and in the meantime, I'll concentrate on serving and pleasing You.

Amen.

May the LORD make it possible for each of you to marry again and have a home.
RUTH 1:9 GNT

God is the best maker of all marriages.

William Shakespeare

MY PERSONAL PRAYER

Dear Father:

_____

_____

_____

_____

_____

_____

_____

Amen

The time and energy that married people spend on caring
for and nurturing each other, the unmarried can spend in
becoming whole and holy instruments of God.
1 CORINTHIANS 7:34 MSG

Let marriage be held in honor (esteemed worthy,
precious, of great price, and especially dear) in all things.
HEBREWS 13:4 AMP

Daily Prayer for help . . . when I've failed

*If I must boast, I would rather boast about
the things that show how weak I am.*
2 CORINTHIANS 11:30 NLT

Dear Heavenly Father,

I blew it—in a big way. It hurts my pride to admit that I failed, but that's exactly what happened. Just when things were going well after graduation and I thought I could do everything on my own, I've been proved wrong. But at least this situation has taught me that I need Your help in every area of my life.

Give me a healthy dose of Your humility and don't let me be so arrogant that I can't learn from this mistake. Thanks for sticking up for me, no matter how big of a mess I made. You always set me back on my feet, and because of Your grace, I know that I'll do better next time.

Amen.

*I am glad to boast about how weak I am; I am glad
to be a living demonstration of Christ's power,
instead of showing off my own power and abilities.*
2 CORINTHIANS 12:9–10 TLB

Those who try and fail are much wiser than those who never try for fear of failure.

André Bustanoby

MY PERSONAL PRAYER

Dear Father:

_____

_____

_____

_____

_____

_____

_____

_____

Amen

My health fails; my spirits droop, yet God remains!
He is the strength of my heart; he is mine forever!
PSALM 73:26 TLB

The One who died for us—who was raised to life for us!—is
in the presence of God at this very moment sticking up for us.
ROMANS 8:33 MSG

Daily Prayer for help . . . when I'm angry

Don't stay angry. Don't go to bed angry.
Don't give the Devil that kind of foothold in your life.
EPHESIANS 4:26 MSG

Dear Heavenly Father,

I'm seeing red right now! Someone violated my rights at work, and I'm so angry I can barely see straight. I don't want to let go of my anger, and I certainly don't want to see that person get away with it, but if I stay this furious, I know it will eat me alive!

Since nothing good can come from my anger, please help me to calm down. Let me take a step back from the situation and gain Your perspective before I say or do something foolish—something that I might live to regret. Please show me how to set aside my pride so that I can work toward a quick and peaceful resolution.

Amen.

It is best to listen much, speak little, and not become angry; for anger doesn't make us good, as God demands that we must be.
JAMES 1:19–20 TLB

I will permit no man to narrow and degrade my soul by making me hate him.

Booker T. Washington

MY PERSONAL PRAYER

Dear Father:

_____

_____

_____

_____

_____

_____

_____

_____

Amen

Anger boomerangs. You can spot a fool
by the lumps on his head.
ECCLESIASTES 7:9 MSG

Stupid people express their anger openly,
but sensible people are patient and hold it back.
PROVERBS 29:11 GNT

Daily Prayer for help . . . when I need a job

From the fruit of his words a man shall be satisfied
with good, and the work of a man's hands shall
come back to him [as a harvest].
PROVERBS 12:14 AMP

Dear Heavenly Father,

It's really stressful to be without work—it's hard to pay bills, to pull my own weight, to take care of myself and my own needs, not to mention to be able to help out other people. I've worked hard to get a good education, but now I need to be able to put my education to good use.

I'm doing my best. I'm out there pounding the pavement, polishing my résumé, checking the want ads every day. But I also need Your help and guidance to show me the right doors to knock on. Where would You like me to go today, Lord? Show me the path You want me to take and teach me to depend on You.

Amen.

Skilled workers are always in demand and admired;
they don't take a back seat to anyone.
PROVERBS 22:29 MSG

On God for all events depend;
You cannot want when God's your friend.
Weigh well your part and do your best;
Leave to your Maker all the rest.

Nathaniel Cotton

MY PERSONAL PRAYER

Dear Father:

_____

_____

_____

_____

_____

_____

_____

_____

Amen

*Make it your aim to live a quiet life, to mind your
own business, and to earn your own living.*
1 THESSALONIANS 4:11 GNT

*There is nothing better for a man than to eat
and drink and tell himself that his labor is good.
This is from the hand of God.*
ECCLESIASTES 2:24 NASB

Daily Prayer for help . . . when I need motivation

We ask you—urge is more like it—that you keep on doing what we told you to do to please God, not in a dogged religious plod, but in a living, spirited dance.

1 THESSALONIANS 4:1 MSG

Dear Heavenly Father,

Some days it's hard to keep going, doing what I know You want me to do, but lacking the motivation I had at the start. I'm a great "beginner," Lord, but not as good of a "finisher." Somewhere in the middle, I seem to get bogged down.

Your Spirit within gives me life so that I can carry on and use the knowledge I gained in school. Breathe on me; inspire me again with Your purpose. Teach me how to carry on—even in the long haul when things get tough, boredom sets in, and enthusiasm lags. Rekindle in my heart the excitement I had when I first started this project with You so that I can finish strong.

Amen.

You are not controlled by your sinful nature. You are controlled by the Spirit if you have the Spirit of God living in you.

ROMANS 8:9 NLT

We can do whatever we wish to do provided our wish is strong enough.

Katherine Mansfield

MY PERSONAL PRAYER

Dear Father:

_____

_____

_____

_____

_____

_____

_____

Amen

The Spirit of life in Christ, like a strong wind, has magnificently cleared the air, freeing you from a fated lifetime of brutal tyranny at the hands of sin and death.
ROMANS 8:2 MSG

In Him we live and move and have our being.
ACTS 17:28

Daily Prayer for help . . . when I need to apologize

When he told me how sorry you were about what had happened, and how loyal your love is for me, I was filled with joy!
2 CORINTHIANS 7:7 NLT

Dear Heavenly Father,

When I was a child, apologies were so much easier to make on the school ground. But as an adult, it's hard to admit I'm wrong. It would be so much easier to just let slide what I've said or done, hoping that the person I've wronged won't notice or that I'll be forgiven without an apology.

But Your Holy Spirit has pricked my conscience, and I know that I need to say, "I'm sorry." It may take guts that I don't have, so I'm asking for Your courage. Even though it won't be easy, I'm determined to make things right. Please give me Your words—words of genuine humility—to restore this relationship.

Amen.

Is anyone sorry for sin? Does anyone say,
"What a terrible thing I have done?"
JEREMIAH 8:6 TLB

An apology is the superglue of life. It can repair just about anything.

Lynn Johnston

MY PERSONAL PRAYER

Dear Father:

_____

_____

_____

_____

_____

_____

_____

_____

Amen

Do people fall down and not get up?
Or take the wrong road and then just keep going?
JEREMIAH 8:4 MSG

I'm glad—not that you were upset,
but that you were jarred into turning things around.
2 CORINTHIANS 7:9 MSG

Daily Prayer for help . . . when I need to forgive

Peter came to him and asked, "Lord, how often should I forgive someone who sins against me? Seven times?" "No!" Jesus replied, "seventy times seven!"
MATTHEW 18:21–22 NLT

Dear Heavenly Father,

There are times when I am so offended by what someone has said or done, that I have no desire to forgive. Now that I've graduated and started a new life, I should act like an adult and be more gracious and compassionate. But I can't do it without Your help, even though I'm miserable. This bitterness has driven a wedge between another person and I, whom I know You also love and have forgiven.

You have told me to forgive, so I choose to do so today no matter what my feelings are telling me. Thank You for the forgiveness You have offered me and for Your gracious love that helps me forgive others just as You do.

Amen.

Now is the time to forgive this man and help him back on his feet.
2 CORINTHIANS 2:7–8 MSG

He who cannot forgive others destroys the bridge over which he himself must pass.

George Herbert

MY PERSONAL PRAYER

Dear Father:

_____

_____

_____

_____

_____

_____

_____

Amen

Remember, the Lord forgave you, so you must forgive others.
COLOSSIANS 3:13 NLT

*Jesus prayed, "Father, keep us forgiven
with you and forgiving others."*
LUKE 11:4 MSG

Daily Prayer for help . . . when I feel I don't belong

LORD, I still belong to you; you are holding my right hand.
PSALM 73:23 NLT

Dear Heavenly Father,

I don't feel like I fit in these days. I'm leaving school behind and entering another phase of my life, which is good, but right now it seems like I don't belong in either place. Who would have ever thought I would miss my teachers? Does anybody care what happens to me now?

Remind me, Lord, that my true home is with You—that You have chosen me and I belong to You and Your family. That's the most important place to belong, and learning to fit in with You is the most fulfilling, satisfying thing I could do. As I seek to please You first, please bring friends into my life that will encourage and support my relationship with You.

Amen.

This includes you, called of Jesus Christ
and invited [as you are] to belong to Him.
ROMANS 1:6 AMP

One of the oldest human needs is having someone to wonder where you are when you don't come home at night.

Margaret Mead

MY PERSONAL PRAYER

Dear Father:

_____

_____

_____

_____

_____

_____

_____

_____

Amen

Since we are all one body in Christ, we belong to each other,
and each of us needs all the others.
ROMANS 12:5 NLT

My dear children, you come from God and belong to God.
1 JOHN 4:4 MSG

Daily Prayer for help . . . when I need to confront someone

By speaking the truth in a spirit of love,
we must grow up in every way to Christ.
EPHESIANS 4:15 GNT

Dear Heavenly Father,

I hate confrontation! It's easier to jump out of an airplane or climb Mount Everest. I'd rather do anything than go to the person I need to confront and tell them how I feel. But that would be taking the easy way out, wouldn't it? And I know that's not what You want me to do.

Strengthen my backbone, Lord. Help me to say the things I need to say—in just the right words that will convey the truth, but still express it in love. Please prepare the heart of this person to hear what I have to say. Let my words be Your words. And please help me to stop shaking.

Amen.

Don't secretly hate your neighbor. If you have something
against him, get it out into the open.
LEVITICUS 19:17 MSG

When you avoid confrontation, you are also avoiding healing and reconciliation.

Andrea Garney

MY PERSONAL PRAYER

Dear Father:

_____

_____

_____

_____

_____

_____

_____

_____

Amen

If a fellow believer hurts you, go and tell him—work it out between the two of you. If he listens, you've made a friend.
MATTHEW 18:15 MSG

GOD was not at all pleased with what David had done, and sent Nathan to David.
2 SAMUEL 12:1 MSG

My dearest Lord,
Be thou a bright flame before me,
Be thou a guiding star above me,
Be thou a smooth path beneath me,
Be thou a kindly shepherd behind me,
Today—tonight—and forever.

COLUMBA

Daily Prayers for Guidance . . .

Daily Prayer for guidance . . . when I need to know God better

God says, "When you come looking for me, you'll find me. Yes, when you get serious about finding me and want it more than anything else, I'll make sure you won't be disappointed."
JEREMIAH 29:13–14 MSG

Dear Heavenly Father,

I've spent years of my life studying different subjects like math, science, psychology, literature, and history. I've taken every required course and many that weren't. I've spent years examining the Bible to gain as much knowledge as I could about Your Word. But these studies pale in comparison to what I really want to know—more about You. The kind of knowledge I want can only come from spending time with You, by searching for You and drawing near to Your heart.

As I seek Your face, Lord, please show me more of You and how wonderful and amazing You are. Getting to know You and love You more is the most important "course" I'll ever take.

Amen.

He makes his thoughts known to man;
this is his name: the LORD God Almighty!
AMOS 4:13 GNT

God warms his hands at man's heart when he prays.
John Mansfield

MY PERSONAL PRAYER

Dear Father:

_____

_____

_____

_____

_____

_____

_____

_____

Amen

> *The LORD still waits for you to come to him*
> *so he can show you his love and compassion.*
> ISAIAH 30:18 NLT

> *Draw close to God, and God will draw close to you.*
> JAMES 4:8 NLT

Daily Prayer for guidance . . . when I need to make a wise decision

You will hear his voice behind you saying,
"Here is the road. Follow it."
ISAIAH 30:21 GNT

Dear Heavenly Father,

What an amazing, confusing, mind-spinning time of life this is! I've finally finished my education, but now I'm faced with so many big decisions. I'm almost paralyzed with the realization of the importance of my upcoming choices.

So just like Solomon did so long ago, I'm asking for Your wisdom. I don't always know what to do, but You know what's best for me, and I know You want me to choose the right road. I'm listening, Lord. Make Your voice ring loud and true! Keep me on the right path, so that my life will bring You glory and honor.

Amen.

God gives wisdom, knowledge,
and happiness to those who please him.
ECCLESIASTES 2:26 GNT

To know the will of God is the highest of all wisdom.

Billy Graham

MY PERSONAL PRAYER

Dear Father:

_____

_____

_____

_____

_____

_____

_____

Amen

*Trust GOD from the bottom of your heart; don't try
to figure everything out on your own. Listen for God's voice
in everything you do, everywhere you go; he's the one
who will keep you on track.*
PROVERBS 3:5–6 MSG

*Who are those who fear the LORD?
He will show them the path they should choose.*
PSALM 25:12 NLT

Daily Prayer for guidance . . . when I need to develop gifts and talents

Each one, as a good manager of God's different gifts, must use for the good of others the special gift he has received from God.
1 PETER 4:10 GNT

Dear Heavenly Father,

I'm about to head out into the world, and I must confess, I'm a little nervous. I've studied hard and tried to determine what my gifts and talents are, but now is the time when I'll find out what I'm really made of.

Whatever I do, I want to make You proud. I want to develop every ability You've given me to bring Your love and joy to other people. I want to bring You glory with my life, so please help me discover every special talent and gift You've placed inside of me and show me how to use them. Bless my efforts, Lord, and help me make an impact on humanity.

Amen.

God's gifts and God's call are under full warranty— never canceled, never rescinded.
ROMANS 11:29 MSG

The same man cannot be skilled in everything; each has his special excellence.

Euripedes

MY PERSONAL PRAYER

Dear Father:

_____

_____

_____

_____

_____

_____

_____

Amen

Earnestly desire and zealously cultivate the greatest and best gifts and graces.
1 CORINTHIANS 12:31 AMP

God said, "I've filled him with the Spirit of God, giving him skill and know-how and expertise."
EXODUS 31:3 MSG

Daily Prayer for guidance . . . when I need to show more love

If I speak with human eloquence and angelic ecstasy
but don't love, I'm nothing but the creaking of a rusty gate.
1 CORINTHIANS 13:1 MSG

Dear Heavenly Father,

I've been a creaky, rusty gate lately—doing all the right things, but with an attitude that is sorely lacking in love. People have been getting on my case, getting in the way, getting on my nerves, and I've been short-tempered and irritable with those around me. Maybe it's because I'm so unsure of myself since leaving school. Whatever the cause, please help me to change.

I remember now that all of the "good" things I do for You actually count as nothing if I'm not sharing Your love with the people You've placed in my life. Please forgive my attitude and fill my heart with love, kindness, and consideration for everyone I meet.

Amen.

Don't just pretend that you love others. Really love them.
ROMANS 12:9 NLT

To love is to make of one's heart a swinging door.

Howard Thurman

MY PERSONAL PRAYER

Dear Father:

_____

_____

_____

_____

_____

_____

_____

Amen

Go after a life of love as if your life depended on it—
because it does.
1 CORINTHIANS 14:1 MSG

Live a life filled with love for others.
EPHESIANS 5:2 NLT

Daily Prayer for guidance . . . when I want to be more generous

Give generously to others in need.
EPHESIANS 4:28 NLT

Dear Heavenly Father,

You own absolutely everything in this world and generously let us use all that You created. It's so hard to freely open up my hands and let go of money or possessions, especially when I've worked hard to earn them. But everything that I have is a gift from You, and all You ask in return is that I give to others.

Help me to remember that it's only because of You that I finished my education. Expand my heart and prevent me from developing a stingy, Grinch-like spirit, Lord. Show me see the opportunities to give that are all around me, and let me use wisdom in my giving. I long to be extravagant with Your amazing gifts!

Amen.

*Do good . . . be rich in helping others . . .
be extravagantly generous.*
1 TIMOTHY 6:18–19 MSG

You cannot outgive God.

Billy Graham

MY PERSONAL PRAYER

Dear Father:

_____

_____

_____

_____

_____

_____

_____

Amen

*Many will give glory to God for your generosity
in sharing with them and everyone else.*
1 CORINTHIANS 9:13 GNT

*Wicked borrows and never returns; righteous gives and gives.
Generous gets it all in the end; stingy is cut off at the pass.*
PSALM 37:21–22 MSG

Daily Prayer for guidance . . . when I want to make better choices

When I want to do what is right, I inevitably do what is wrong. Oh, what a miserable person I am! Who will free me from this life that is dominated by sin? Thank God! The answer is in Jesus Christ our Lord.
ROMANS 7:21, 24–25 NLT

Dear Heavenly Father,

I know exactly how the Apostle Paul felt when he said he wanted to do the right things, but somehow he kept doing what was wrong! Why is it so hard to make the right choices—to do what I know would be pleasing to You? I'm constantly fighting within myself, wanting to go my own way. Now that I've graduated, there are so many tempting roads to take.

Life is so much easier when I listen to Your directions and am obedient to Your will. Lord, I choose to follow You for the rest of my life, but when I make a wrong turn, let Your light show me how to get back on track.

Amen.

Now that you've found you don't have to listen to sin tell you what to do, and have discovered the delight of listening to God telling you, what a surprise!
ROMANS 6:22 MSG

To have a right to do a thing is not at all the same as to be right in doing it.

G. K. Chesterton

MY PERSONAL PRAYER

Dear Father:

_____

_____

_____

_____

_____

_____

_____

Amen

*Choose to love the Lord your God and to obey him
and commit yourself to him, for he is your life.*
DEUTERONOMY 30:20 NLT

We should choose to follow what is right.
JOB 34:4 TLB

Daily Prayer for guidance . . . when I want to tell others about God

*Those who put others on the right path
to life will glow like stars forever.*
DANIEL 12:3 MSG

Dear Heavenly Father,

You're the best! Everybody needs to know how wonderful You are! You've given me the incredible privilege of sharing with school friends the amazing things You've done for me, but sometimes I get nervous, afraid that I'll say the wrong thing, that I'll embarrass myself or You, or that people will laugh at what I have to say.

Please send Your Holy Spirit ahead of me to prepare the hearts of those I'll encounter after graduation. Only You can draw them to Yourself. Then shine through me—both through my words and my life—and make me a walking, talking, smiling, sharing, laughing, loving ambassador of Christ!

Amen.

*The signs and wonders that the Most High God
has worked for me I am pleased to recount.*
DANIEL 4:2 NRSV

It is no use walking anywhere to preach unless we preach as we walk.

Saint Francis of Assisi

MY PERSONAL PRAYER

Dear Father:

_____

_____

_____

_____

_____

_____

_____

Amen

Give thanks to the LORD! Tell all the nations
what he has done! Tell them how great he is!
ISAIAH 12:4 GNT

GOD, I'll tell the world how great and good you are.
I'll shout Hallelujah all day, every day.
PSALM 35:28 MSG

Daily Prayer for guidance . . . when I want to mend a relationship

God settled the relationship between us and him, and then called us to settle our relationships with each other.
2 CORINTHIANS 5:18 MSG

Dear Heavenly Father,

I'm not sure how the relationship with my friend went from good to bad to worse. One of us said something, one of us took it the wrong way, we've hurt each other, and I'm worried that things will never be the same. And now that we've graduated, it's even harder to stay close.

What can I do to make our relationship right again? I really need Your wisdom and love in this situation. Please give me the right words to say—and help my friend listen to my heart when I say them. You are the great Reconciler, the great Forgiver, the great Restorer of relationships. Help me be more like You.

Amen.

What a joy it is to find just the right word for the right occasion!
PROVERBS 15:23 GNT

Forgiveness is the fragrance the violet sheds on the heel that has crushed it.

Mark Twain

MY PERSONAL PRAYER

Dear Father:

_____
_____
_____
_____
_____
_____
_____
_____

Amen

If you want people to like you, forgive them when they wrong you. Remembering wrongs can break up a friendship.
PROVERBS 17:9 GNT

Hatred stirs old quarrels, but love overlooks insults.
PROVERBS 10:12 TLB

Praise God, from whom all blessings flow;
Praise him, all creatures here below;
Praise him above ye heavenly host;
Praise Father, Son and Holy Ghost.

THOMAS KEN

Daily Prayers of Praise . . .

Daily Prayer of praise for . . . life

It is a wonderful thing to be alive!
ECCLESIASTES 11:7 TLB

Dear Heavenly Father,

Your gift of life is so amazing! Just the fact that I've been given eyes to see Your beautiful creation, taste buds to savor delicious foods, ears to hear songs that move my heart, and arms to hold my loved ones close—is overwhelming. Your gifts are too many to count!

I don't tell You 'thank You' nearly often enough. Every day that I wake up is a new day to experience Your mercy, grace, and love. Thank You so much for this challenging, mysterious, grand, and glorious life You have planned for me as a new graduate!

Amen.

You, O LORD, are the fountain of life.
PSALM 36:9 NLT

Every man's life is a fairy tale, written by God's fingers.

Hans Christian Anderson

MY PERSONAL PRAYER

Dear Father:

_____

_____

_____

_____

_____

_____

_____

_____

Amen

*Jesus said, "I came that they can have real and eternal life,
more and better life than they ever dreamed of."*
JOHN 10:10 MSG

*All the stages of my life were spread out before you,
the days of my life all prepared before I'd even lived one day.*
PSALM 139:16 MSG

Daily Prayer of praise for . . .
God's gifts

*Every good gift and every perfect present comes from heaven;
it comes down from God, the Creator of the heavenly lights.*
JAMES 1:17 GNT

Dear Heavenly Father,

You're the greatest Present-Giver ever! Every time I think I've given You a gift, I realize that in return, You have given me a thousand times more. Everything good in my life has passed through Your hands. You shower me with more blessings than I can even count: good friends, a loving family, a wonderful education, a purpose in life, and the ability to fulfill that purpose.

Not only do You give me good gifts in this lifetime, but You're preparing even more blessings for me in heaven. How can I ever thank You enough? It's not possible! But for the rest of my life, I'll continue to praise You!

Amen.

Father, everything I have is a gift from you.
JOHN 17:7 NLT

God gave you a gift of 86,400 seconds today. Have you used one to say "thank you"?

William Arthur Ward

MY PERSONAL PRAYER

Dear Father:

_____

_____

_____

_____

_____

_____

_____

Amen

All who receive God's wonderful, gracious gift
of righteousness will live in triumph over sin and death.
ROMANS 5:17 NLT

Each day is God's gift. Make the most of each one!
ECCLESIASTES 9:9 MSG

Daily Prayer of praise for . . .
God's creation

Sing to GOD a brand-new song. He's made a world of wonders!
PSALM 98:1 MSG

Dear Heavenly Father,

When I look around at the works of Your hands, I realize what a God of infinite variety and imagination You are! Giraffes, hippos, monkeys, toucans—all demonstrate Your creativity and Your humor. Mountains, forests, beaches, waterfalls—all are evidence of Your great power and beauty. Africans, Asians, Native Americans, Hispanics, Europeans—people of every size and color—all show that Your love has no boundaries. Everywhere I look, I see the amazing world You have created. How could anyone not believe in You?

Thank You for everything You've made, Lord, including me. Thank You for my mind, my body, and my spirit. I praise You, my Creator, my God, and my Friend.

Amen.

O LORD, our Lord, your greatness is seen in all the world!
PSALM 8:9 GNT

Everything bears the fingerprints of God.

Richard Carlson

MY PERSONAL PRAYER

Dear Father:

_____

_____

_____

_____

_____

_____

_____

_____

Amen

Be glad; rejoice forever in my creation!
ISAIAH 65:18 NLT

The heavens are yours, O LORD, and the earth is yours;
everything in the world is yours—you created it all.
PSALM 89:11 NLT

Daily Prayer of praise for . . .
good health

*Keep my message in plain view at all times. Concentrate!
Learn it by heart! Those who discover these words live, really
live; body and soul, they're bursting with health.*
PROVERBS 4:21–22 MSG

Dear Heavenly Father,

When I was in school, I often took my body for granted, skipping meals, eating junk food, and staying up too late. I know it can't take that abuse forever. But it's so easy to just take my body for granted, assuming it will always work correctly. I know though that for many people in this world, good health would be the greatest gift they could imagine.

Now that I'm grown, help strengthen my willpower to take better care of my body—this temple of the Holy Spirit. Teach me to honor and cherish the health that You have given me and to always praise You for it.

Amen.

Your heart will rejoice; vigorous health will be yours.
ISAIAH 66:14 TLB

I have good health, good thoughts, and good humor, thanks be to God Almighty.

William Byrd

MY PERSONAL PRAYER

Dear Father:

_____

_____

_____

_____

_____

_____

_____

_____

Amen

You who are young, make the most of your youth.
Relish your youthful vigor!
ECCLESIASTES 11:9 MSG

O LORD my God, you restored my health.
PSALM 30:2 NLT

Daily Prayer of praise for . . .
those I love

Every time you cross my mind,
I break out in exclamations of thanks to God.
PHILIPPIANS 1:3 MSG

Dear Heavenly Father,

What would I do without all of the wonderful people You've placed in my life? My parents and grandparents, brothers, sisters, friends, caretakers, and other loved ones—they're the greatest blessings of all. Each one played an important role in helping me get through school, whether it was a word of wisdom, the gift of laughter, or discipline when I needed it.

Lord, please show me ways that I can bless my family and friends. Remind me to tell them of my love more often. Just as You have blessed me, I want to be a blessing and an example of Your heart. Lord, I give You praise and honor and glory for those I love.

Amen.

We always give thanks to God, the Father of
our Lord Jesus Christ, when we pray for you.
COLOSSIANS 1:3 GNT

Make no mistake about it, responsibilities toward other human beings are the greatest blessings God can send us.

Dorothy Dix

MY PERSONAL PRAYER

Dear Father:

_____

_____

_____

_____

_____

_____

_____

_____

Amen

Just as lotions and fragrance give sensual delight,
a sweet friendship refreshes the soul.
PROVERBS 27:9 MSG

If we walk in the light, we experience
a shared life with one another.
1 JOHN 1:7 MSG

Daily Prayer of praise for . . . how God created me

Thank you for making me so wonderfully complex! It is amazing to think about. Your workmanship is marvelous.
PSALM 139:14 TLB

Dear Heavenly Father,

I must confess, I'm not always thrilled about what I see when I look in the mirror. It was so hard when I was in school because my peers made me conscious of every flaw. Will it be that way when I leave behind campus life and enter the working world? Yet I must admit I'm often my toughest critic, forgetting that You are the One who made me, and You like me just the way I am.

My mind and body are truly amazing when I think about it. You've placed Your image on me, Your glory inside of me, and I'm so grateful for what You've given. Help me to always praise You for how You created me.

Amen.

God said, "Before I shaped you in the womb, I knew all about you. Before you saw the light of day, I had holy plans for you."
JEREMIAH 1:5 MSG

We were born to make manifest the glory of God that is within us. It's not just in some of us, it's in everyone.

Nelson Mandela

MY PERSONAL PRAYER

Dear Father:

_____

_____

_____

_____

_____

_____

_____

Amen

God created people in his own image;
God patterned them after himself.
GENESIS 1:27 NLT

God formed Man out of dirt from the ground
and blew into his nostrils the breath of life.
The Man came alive—a living soul!
GENESIS 2:7 MSG

Daily Prayer of praise for . . .
unexpected blessings

*We praise God for the wonderful kindness he has
poured out on us because we belong to his dearly loved Son.*
EPHESIANS 1:6 NLT

Dear Heavenly Father,

Wow, Lord! You really surprised me with Your latest blessing. Graduating would have been enough, but You have given me new insight into myself and Your plan for me. God, You are truly amazing! I can't seem to go a day now without You pouring new ideas into my head or opening a door for the future.

Thank You for all You are doing behind the scenes that I don't always see. How can I ever repay You for what You have done in my life? I'll always love You, praise You, and obey You—not because I have to, but because You have made it such a joy to follow You!

Amen.

*Blessings in the city, blessings in the field; many children,
ample crops, large flocks and herds; blessings of fruit and
bread; blessings when you come in, blessings when you go out.*
DEUTERONOMY 28:2 TLB

Be glad of life because it gives you the chance to love and to work and to play and to look up at the stars.

Henry Van Dyke

MY PERSONAL PRAYER

Dear Father:

_____

_____

_____

_____

_____

_____

_____

Amen

Lord, you have poured out amazing blessings on this land!
PSALM 85:1 TLB

My cup brims with blessing.
PSALM 23:5 MSG

Daily Prayer of praise for . . .
God's love

Praise the LORD, for he has shown me his unfailing love.
PSALM 31:21 NLT

Dear Heavenly Father,

Long before I was born, even before the creation of the world, You knew who I would become—and You loved me. You nurtured me, educated me, and laid out a perfect plan for my life. Best of all, You sent Your Son to the cross to die for me, when You knew I would need Your salvation to be able to spend eternity with You.

I'm so grateful that Your love and approval isn't the human, fickle kind of love—based on the good things that I do, the good grades that I get, or even the love that I give You in return. No, Your amazing love is unconditional and will never end. Praise You, Lord!

Amen.

We know how much God loves us,
and we have put our trust in him.
1 JOHN 4:16 NLT

God hears no sweeter music than the cracked chimes of the courageous human spirit ringing in imperfect acknowledgment of His perfect love.

Joshua Loth Liebman

MY PERSONAL PRAYER

Dear Father:

_____

_____

_____

_____

_____

_____

_____

_____

Amen

God is love.
1 JOHN 4:8 NLT

This is what love is: it is not that we have loved God,
but that he loved us.
1 JOHN 4:10 GNT

Daily Prayer of praise for . . . eternal life

*God's gift is real life, eternal life,
delivered by Jesus, our Master.*
ROMANS 6:23 MSG

Dear Heavenly Father,

This life is not all there is. It's not always easy to remember that in the hectic schedules and demands I'm facing after graduation—but it's the truth! There's an even greater life for me in the future, and I'm so grateful that You've saved me from death and will allow me to spend all of eternity praising and worshiping You.

Lord, You loved me so much that You made a way for me to live forever. You didn't have to—but I'm so glad You did! Because of Your great love for me, even though my body will one day grow old and pass away, I will live forever! Hallelujah!

Amen.

God has given us eternal life, and this life is in His Son.
1 JOHN 5:11

The truest end of life is to know the life that never ends.
William Penn

MY PERSONAL PRAYER

Dear Father:

_____

_____

_____

_____

_____

_____

_____

Amen

Your goodness and unfailing kindness shall be with me
all of my life, and afterwards I will live with you
forever in your home.
PSALM 23:6 TLB

You canceled my ticket to hell—that's not my destination!
Now you've got my feet on the life path, all radiant
from the shining of your face.
PSALM 16:10–11 MSG

Daily Prayer of praise for . . . heaven

God will wipe away all tears from their eyes.
There will be no more death, no more grief or crying or pain.
The old things have disappeared.
REVELATION 21:4 GNT

Dear Heavenly Father,

It's so hard to imagine what heaven will be like—streets of gold, a bright city filled with light, loved ones who have gone on to be with You. Praise You for making heaven possible through the gift of Your Son! No more death, pain, crying, or fear. The thought of spending eternity in Your presence brings me more joy than I can express.

As I live the rest of my life, help me always to remember that heaven is my home. Someday I'll see You face to face and move into the magnificent mansion that You're preparing for me. I may not know much about heaven, but I do know that I will love it because You are there!

Amen.

You will keep on guiding me all my life with your wisdom and counsel; and afterwards receive me into the glories of heaven!
PSALM 73:24 TLB

Earth has no sorrow that heaven cannot heal.

Thomas Moore

MY PERSONAL PRAYER

Dear Father:

_____

_____

_____

_____

_____

_____

_____

Amen

*You should have as little desire for this world as a dead person
does. Your real life is in heaven with Christ and God.*
COLOSSIANS 3:3 TLB

*The Spirit of God whets our appetite by giving us a taste
of what's ahead. He puts a little heaven in our hearts
so that we'll never settle for less.*
2 CORINTHIANS 5:4–5 MSG

Topical Reference Index

For additions, deletions, corrections or clarifications
in future editions of this text, please e-mail
ContactUs@ElmHillBooks.com.

....

Products from Elm Hill Books may be purchased in
bulk for educational, business, fundraising, or sales
promotional use. For information, please email
SpecialMarkets@ThomasNelson.com.

....

Additional copies of this book and other titles from
ELM HILL BOOKS are available from your local bookstore.

Mercy abundantly given
Help for the difficult place
Courage when it's sorely needed,
Strength for the problems we face!
Comfort when grief assails us,
Love when we need someone to care
These are the blessings of God
That He gives in answer to prayer!

—Mary D. Hughes